BREAKING THE CYCLE

SURVIVORS OF CHILD ABUSE AND NEGLECT

PAMELA FONG

BREAKING THE CYCLE

SURVIVORS OF CHILD ABUSE
AND NEGLECT

ESSAY BY ROBERT COLES

W.W. NORTON & COMPANY
NEW YORK · LONDON

First Edition

Designed by Katy Homans
Typeset in Gill Sans by Trufont Typographers
Printed in Hong Kong by South China Printing

Library of Congress Cataloging-in-Publication Data

Fong, Pamela J.
Breaking the cycle : survivors of child abuse and neglect / Pamela Fong : with an essay by Robert Coles.
p.   cm.
Includes index.
ISBN 0-393-02979-4
1. Adult child abuse victims—United States—Pictorial works.
2. Adult child sexual abuse victims—United States—Pictorial works.
I. Coles, Robert.   II. Title.
HV6626.5.F65   1991
362.7'6—dc20   90-22878
CIP

ISBN: 0-393-02979-4
ISBN: 0-393-30789-1 PBK

W.W. Norton & Company, Inc., 500 Fifth Avenue, New York, N.Y. 10110
W.W. Norton & Company, Ltd., 10 Coptic Street, London WC1A 1PU
1 2 3 4 5 6 7 8 9 0

CONTENTS

ACKNOWLEDGMENTS

With great respect, admiration and gratitude, this book is dedicated to the survivors and their families who have had the courage to participate in this project. For the sake of protecting their anonymity, I regret that I cannot name the individuals who have collaborated with me to develop this book. Many of the children are in the protective custody of their single parents or have otherwise been removed from the danger of the offender.

We are fortunate to have a large network of clinicians and legal professionals who dedicate their lives to protect, heal and work with survivors, intervening as early as possible in an effort to break the cycle of abuse from generation to generation. Their generosity, confidence and good counsel have been a constant source of support and inspiration. I would in particular like to mention Nikki Alexander, Kevin Boshea, Linda Conner, Dave Denson, Michael Durfee, Joan Suzuki Hart, Tamara Kreinin, Margaret Ready, Donna Rosenberg, Robert Stuckey, Roland Summit, Marly Sweeney and Valerie Wolf.

It is a great privilege to have the quiet, eloquent, personal essay by Robert Coles introduce the viewer to the people in the photographs. His prolific lifetime involvement with children in crises is extraordinary. And I am grateful that he carved out the time to address some of the issues of the present volume.

Howard Spector helped me shape the narrative of the images and cull down the number of prints. His curatorial assistance and friendship have been invaluable.

At W. W. Norton, my editor, Jim Mairs, has been a steady source of guidance and renewal of spirit, and he took the chance to do this project. After losing their hearts to the children in the initial set of photographs, Rick Raeber, Oliver Gilliland and Susan Bengel have continued to rally behind the book, which made it a possibility.

I appreciate the enthusiasm and care with which Cecil Lyon and Eve Picower, assistant editors at W. W. Norton, have worked with the constantly growing materials. And I would like to thank designer Katy Homans for the clean, elegant lines of the book.

In its early stages, Glenn Goldman was very instrumental in generating support for the project. After poring over the voluminous transcripts and proof sheets, Margo Chase offered her delicate vision.

My dear friends Mie and Michael Hunt Collins, Shirley Schackmann, and Roger Simon, have worked with me over the last three years to develop the structure of the book and edit the images and text. Their emotional support and good humor during some of the particularly spiny times continue to surprise and delight me.

And finally, I would like to thank my family and friends for their unconditional love. And Jack.

PREFACE

On an airplane four years ago, I happened to sit next to a woman named Donna Rosenberg. She is a dedicated pediatrician working on a child protection team at a well-known child abuse center. She told me about a brutally raped two-year-old girl who had been brought in by her father. He had said simply, "She's bleeding."

I thought of my two-year-old niece, who had just recently learned to walk and speak, and it was difficult for me to imagine such a thing. The vision of this bleeding child continued to haunt me for two years during which I stayed in contact with Donna, sending her portfolios and proposals in an effort to persuade her that I was seriously interested in photographing some of these children and their families. Only through developing her trust would I be able to gain access to the very protective network of clinicians through whom I hoped to contact survivors.

I didn't know what to expect when I finally started meeting survivors and their families. But what became immediately apparent as I made my way across the United States, crossing racial and socioeconomic boundaries, was how familiar everyone seemed. These were families we've all seen in our own neighborhoods, ordinary people we meet at the grocery store or walking the dog.

And as I heard their stories and those of other people I'd meet each day, at the hardware store or while dining at a friend's house, I realized not only how pervasive child abuse is but how in some way, we all carry with us our own dark areas of pain and feelings of abuse, some more extreme than others. So these photographs in a sense became pictures of all of us.

I was impressed by the courage and hope some of the adult survivors had after living for so long with unabating pain and betrayal. While speaking with a group of twenty-six incest survivors, I was stunned by the fact that many of them could not even remember the abuse until they were in their mid-thirties.

A disproportionate number of the adults in this essay are women. It was difficult to gain access to the male survivor population. Several clinicians suggested that it is harder for male survivors to deal publically with histories of abuse. Traditionally men have not been encouraged to express themselves in the same manner as women. Moreover, when a man has a history of sexual abuse, there are more social taboos to overcome. Not only is a boy supposed to be "tough" enough to take care of himself, but if he has been sexually violated, quite often that molestation is homosexual.

Also the concept of what constitutes a family was changing and when there was a typical nuclear family working on abuse issues, the father often decided not to take part in the project.

While looking at the people in these photographs you may wonder what happened in each situation. I was originally going to include a brief history of each family with quotes from the hundred interviews I taped. But I considered it more important to protect the privacy of these individuals, especially the children, with regard to the often secretive details of the abuse, and not to perpetuate an already abusive pattern in their lives. Instead, some of these quotes have been placed in the back of the book.

The children in this essay are either survivors, or children of survivors, or sometimes survivors of abuse by people outside of the family.

You will see no physical evidence of abuse in these photographs. All of these people are working toward breaking the cycle of abuse, and I chose to show them not as victims, but as survivors.

PAMELA FONG
November 1990

THE ASSAULT ON A CHILD

ROBERT COLES

During my years of training in psychoanalytic child psychiatry I elected to do clinical work with "juvenile delinquents," youths who had gotten into trouble with the law, youths who were in difficulty psychologically and had a hard time keeping their problems to themselves, so to speak. These boys and girls fought with others, insulted teachers (in school, in the neighborhood), even without provocation. Sometimes these youngsters were so angry, so hard to reason with, so inclined to take offense and get into trouble, that they had to be removed from their homes and remanded by the courts to state-run institutions, called industrial schools in Massachusetts as recently as the 1960s.

For two years I was a psychiatric consultant to one of those industrial schools, in Lancaster, Massachusetts, with over a hundred quite agitated, often truculent, sometimes quite depressed—even suicidal—girls and young women. I talked with many of them in groups, and I got to know some of them, who became my patients, as individuals. Week after week we had staff conferences, and occasionally distinguished child psychoanalysts came to talk with us, to listen as we presented our cases. Once Fritz Redl, who had spent a lifetime working with troubled young people, addressed us, and I had the privilege of discussing with him an especially disturbed girl of twelve, Jean, who already had a substantial legal history of assault and battery charges, a relatively rare phenomenon among women of any age, let alone one so young. I had spent weeks trying to earn the confidence of this sullen, morose girl, but she had not been forthcoming with me—nor with the nurses, her social worker, a woman pediatrician, and a woman psychiatrist whom I'd asked to come and help us all, on the assumption that Jean would find it easier to talk with someone of her own sex.

None of us had much to report about Jean's early life. She had confined her remarks mostly to truculent defenses about her "side" of the various arguments she'd had with this or that person. In giving reasons for her inclination to take people on physically, strike a punch here, let go with a kick there, she was forthright and even blunt: "Lots of people, they are tricky and they are out to hurt you, and I have learned to keep my eyes open, and if I see them looking for trouble, then I just defend myself as best I can."

I'd heard her talk like that many times. But when I asked her why she was so constantly wary of people, so quick to regard the world as overbearing, if not personally antagonistic to her, she would become reluctant to speak or even stubbornly silent. My own response was then to call her (to myself, in the notes I wrote on her record) by various clinical names, such as "paranoid" and even "sociopathic," because she had conspired with others to assault certain girls in the institution, and had stolen money at home and from a teacher before her admission.

When Dr. Redl had heard me tell what I knew of Jean, he asked if he might interview her. Certainly, we all said—if she was willing. She was not all that willing, but she assented. I knew she'd soon reveal how reluctant she was to talk about herself, and indeed for a while, as Dr. Redl talked with her, we heard nothing much: his questions were brusquely parried or met with a brief yes or no. Finally, Dr. Redl seemed defeated—prepared to end the interview. I was frustrated; I had hoped that someone, somehow, would find out more about this tough young woman, who in her own way was terrorizing an institution meant to care for people like herself. But now this distinguished psychoanalyst was saying thanks to Jean for coming to talk with him, he having been no more able to get at the source of her angry, defiant, threatening manner than the rest of us. Jean stood up, and with her, Dr. Redl. Suddenly, he looked right at her; he didn't ask her another question, but made a statement: "You know, in my long life working with young people I have learned that those who scare others have been scared badly themselves—and those who attack others have been attacked and attacked and attacked themselves."

Jean stood there—now silent, rather than quick to respond, as she had been earlier. We were all wondering what would happen next, and why Dr. Redl had used the verb *attacked* three times. I can still hear him doing so, and can still remember thinking that I had not heard from Jean any account of abuse by her parents, whom she had described repeatedly as ordinary, decent people, the stepfather a salesman in a Sears, Roebuck store, the mother a housewife. (Jean had two younger brothers, both then apparently without major psychiatric troubles.) Finally, the girl spoke: "Doctor, are you trying to say something?"

The doctor said nothing; rather, he simply nodded his head. Jean looked down at the floor, not for a second, but long enough for all of us to become nervous. Eventually Dr. Redl felt the need to say something, to rescue her eyes from their unyieldingly downward direction: "What are you thinking?" The old standby for us in psychiatry! I knew Jean well enough to be immediately apprehensive. To this day I can hear her answer—because I will never forget how I anticipated that answer, word for word, a second or so before it was spoken, not out of clairvoyance, but because I myself had posed such a question several times to this feisty, quick-tempered young person, and had been called to account by her response: "Well, what are *you* thinking?"

When Jean had put such a wall between herself and me, between my inquiry and her life, I had quickly relented, tried to change tack. But Dr. Redl was far more self-assured, and far more willing to force matters to a (clarifying, he hoped) confrontation—after which, of course, he would leave for his next speaking destination, while Jean and the rest of us would try to take up from there! "I am thinking," he told Jean, "that you know why I asked that question, and you want to answer it, but you also don't want to answer it."

I noted how careful Dr. Redl was, how restrained, too: he made no effort at that moment to pin a patronizing psychiatric designation on this patient—to tell her she was "afraid" to answer the question, or was made "anxious" by it. Now I was shifting my bets. At first I had given low odds that Jean would respond cooperatively to the doctor's interest in her past, but I was beginning to sense a responsive turn on her part. For one thing, she looked up and let her eyes meet the doctor's. Moreover, she seemed quiet and thoughtful, not the irritable, agitated Jean I knew so well. Finally her face formed the thinnest of smiles—her way of announcing, before a word was spoken, that she was ready to work with this elderly stranger; and then, this: "My father beat me up regularly." A brief pause was followed by an amplification: "He wasn't my real father."

The doctor was obviously not surprised by what he heard, nor unprepared to pursue its significance. He sat down, and she with him, and they engaged in a serious and sustained conversation. He encouraged her to describe at least some of what she had experienced as a child, and she did so—much to the surprise of us who knew her so well, and as we heard certain details, much to our horror as well. Here was a young woman, we began to realize, who had been relentlessly hit, and relentlessly abused sexually, by a man her mother lived with but never married. (Jean's biological father had been killed in an automobile accident when she was four years old; he had been drinking heavily, and lost control of his car.) As this sad story unfolded, an adolescent girl's troublesome behavior was suddenly revealed for what it was—a mirror of what she had for years endured. When we had heard this story, when Jean sat back, obviously exhausted by what she had remembered and relayed, I wondered how Dr. Redl would bring this startling and horrifying interview to a conclusion. He seemed quite touched by what he had heard—had elicited. He was silent for a few moments and seemed to hesitate, as if all too inconclusively asking himself, as we had been asking, what could be said at this point? Finally, he leaned forward just a bit, and with a gentle, kindly voice delivered a message to Jean: "I guess that is what we do: when we have been hurt by others, we become their victims, and we even become like them in the long run, because what they have done to us won't let go—it just won't."

I can still hear him as he spoke, and especially I can hear him pausing toward the end, just before those last three words. He intended to point something out to Jean in such a way that she felt connected to others, a part of the human scene, rather than some freak who had been dealt a bad hand by fate, or worse, a young sinner who had committed repeated crimes and therefore bore a moral mark that would not disappear. And he succeeded, we began to realize soon enough; Jean smiled at him after hearing his message, and that day was subdued, reflective, even pleasant to the staff, rather than the difficult, demanding, constantly aggressive person we had all known for so long.

I am not trying to say that this dramatic moment resulted in a complete change in an extremely troubled young life, or even a modest change in the tone of Jean's behavior, the manner in which she engaged with others. We had plenty of the old Jean to confront, to challenge with our psychiatric rationality (and no doubt, our flawed understanding). But now she was at least willing to talk with us about her actions, and even more important, about her earlier life, a subject hitherto a firmly closed book. In the weeks after that clinical conference—that turning point, really, for her and for me as her day-to-day doctor—I learned many of the details of Jean's early life: a childhood of constant vulnerability, constant injury, constant terror. The more I heard, the better I understood her youthful rages—their meaning to her. She had been terribly mistreated, and her mother had never intervened (when the girl many times had dared say she had something to "tell," she was simply told not to be a "complainer"). No wonder she had no real trust in people, and was constantly afraid that someone, anyone, would—as she so often said—"trick" or "double-cross" her. No wonder she went on the attack so frequently. Had she not done so, I slowly realized, she would have fallen into a serious depression. Indeed, a month or so after Dr. Redl's visit, she became increasingly melancholy, withdrawn, uncommunicative. She told me, one day, that she wished she were her old tough self, quick to express anger, ready in a flash to test and tease people and even throw a punch or two at them. "This is the pits," she told me—and that statement was for her an unusual admission of weakness, an unusual step in her progress toward self-observation. More and more, thereafter, she returned to her earlier years, and alas, to the awful events of that time.

It was from her that I learned much about what we now call child abuse and sexual abuse, neither of them then (the late 1950s) a prominent "subject." Once she got started talking, Jean was at pains to let me know a lot, and I will admit that there were moments when I wondered whether she wasn't exaggerating or embellishing her narrative statements, her memories, her descriptions of what she had had to endure at the hands of a so-called stepfather, not to mention a mother who drank too much and thereby avoided facing up to a lot that she may have suspected. I would now and then try gently, tactfully, to call Jean to account: to check certain details, to ask whether she was "sure" that this man she was describing was "actually" quite the brutish and assaultive individual she presented him as being. I have to admit, I even wondered (as Freud had wondered, as we in psychoanalytic training were taught to wonder) whether much of what Jean described wasn't the result of a vigorous imagination constantly at work. Once, I fear, I used that word *actually* in such a way that Jean took offense. She asked, "Do you doubt me?" Quickly I replied no—but she perceived otherwise on my face, and I realized later, in my voice. "You *do* doubt me," she averred, and I said nothing, whereupon (a critjcial moment in the time we spent together) she said this to me: "I don't blame you. I don't want to believe it happened, I don't. For a long time I'd say it *didn't* happen. I kept remembering the way he'd come and grab me, and if I tried to get away, he'd hit me, and if I still tried, he'd hit me harder; and then I'd give up, and then he'd start in with all that stuff he'd do, and I'd try to think I was dead, that's what. I'd keep saying to myself that I was dead and gone; and when I wasn't thinking that, there was something else I'd think; I'd think that there's a God, they'd tell us in church. So He must be seeing all this, and He'll remember, if I don't, and He's stronger than *him*, and *he'll* meet Him, one of these days he will, and that'll be the end of *him*, that's what will happen. I'd keep thinking that; I'd keep talking to God: 'Please, help me out, and if You can't now, do something later to this man.' That's what I thought."

Such a rendering by Jean of her past thoughts more than convinced me. Certainly the psychoanalytic supervisor to whom I reported my work with Jean was more than persuaded of her earnest veracity. He kept encouraging me to encourage Jean to talk about how she felt before, during, and after the beatings, the sexual assaults—but she kept returning to those twin responses, that she felt "dead" and that she turned to God, in her own desperate and idiosyncratic way. As for the "details" of what had happened to her (my supervisor pressed me to find them out), Jean was willing—I later realized—to be more forthcoming that I was prepared for her to be.

At that time we child psychiatrists were unfamiliar with such happenings—and doctors were not alert, in emergency rooms, to the telltale clinical signs of their likely presence in this or that child's life. I remember my time of emergency-room duty as a pediatric intern (in Boston's Children's Hospital) some years earlier, and I remember the children whose arms and legs and torsos and skulls we X-rayed, whose black-and-blue skin we observed, whose darkened eye sockets we noted—and always those explanations, those farfetched tales, those out-and-out lies, I now say with no hesitation. What I remember, too, is the occasional hard look exchanged between me and another doctor or a nurse—as if to say, Lord, this is terrible, and criminal. Yet we felt so helpless. Always I'd call a senior pediatric resident, or even an attending physician, and always, it seemed, we cowered before the legal nightmare that loomed, we knew, if we sought to challenge those parents with their insistent accounts of exactly what had happened and why.

Only once during my time in the emergency room did the usual medical timidity and passivity give way to a concerted effort to explore the reasons for a child's serious injuries. An eight-year-old boy came in with bad bruises on the back and buttocks, all attributed by his mother and stepfather to a "neighborhood fight." Preposterous, several of us thought—even as the boy echoed the claims of those two adults in his life, while we tried to tend to his injuries. A couple of hours later, as the boy and his parents prepared to leave, the mother suddenly started crying in front of us, two young doctors and a nurse. We asked her what was wrong. "Nothing," she said. But still she cried; and her tears soon prompted the boy to start crying. We asked him what was wrong—and once again were told, "Nothing." I remember looking at the stepfather and thinking to myself, *he'll* not cry! I remember, too, staring at his hands—as if trying to say something (to myself, never mind to him) through such a fixation of vision. I stared long enough for the man to put his arms behind his back—and meanwhile, my fellow pediatric intern was signaling to me with his eyes to move to a room where we could have a further discussion.

Eventually, the mother broke down further and told us what had "really" happened, what by then we knew had happened. Her husband hurriedly left the hospital, ostensibly to keep an appointment. We learned later that he did, in fact, keep an appointment, with a lawyer. We expected to be appearing in court, for the mother too consulted a lawyer and he in turn talked with us. But several weeks later, the mother dropped the charges and, we would learn, left the state with her husband and son. All of us in the hospital had our private visions about what would happen to that boy in the years ahead—the visits to the various hospitals that would follow the beatings; or maybe, fewer hospital visits, because the danger of exposure and possible court action had now been made real to a violent man who "had it in for" his stepson, so the child's mother told us. As for her psychology—why she stayed with this man, and essentially, offered her son to his abusive inclination—we could only speculate, conjecturing about the nature of her "masochism" or her "ambivalence" toward this son born out of wedlock and resembling his biological father, who had left her early on.

Even Jean, whom we all got to know far better than that boy and his mother, and whom Dr. Redl had confronted so tellingly, did not stay with us long enough for any real discovery to be made on her part or ours as to the psychological sources of the abuse she sustained. Had she been with us longer, we might have learned a lot more not only about her but about the adults who figured so tragically, destructively, in her life. Dr. Redl had made an end run around her fiercely self-protective ways of sealing off the past's terrible injuries. But in almost no time, despite our hard work to take advantage of what had happened during the last minutes of that staff conference, Jean was demanding to be released, with a real sense of urgency that translated into good everyday behavior. Having come to realize that the worse she acted, the more "antisocial," the longer she would have to stay, she made herself a model of cooperative affability—obviously to speed up her release. "I know you folks want to keep me here and figure me out," she kept telling us—but she went no further. We were forced to recognize that a few moments of "insight" had not only awakened her to her past difficulties, her afflictions, but also frightened her badly; we saw that she wanted "out," as she now told us with new conviction, because she feared ever so much the prospect of a careful, sustained look at what had happened to her and at what, in response, she had figured out to do—her manner of dealing with those awful accumulated experiences. For her, alas, the alternative was a swift exit. Nor were we her keepers. Once her "delinquent" manner subsided, we were quite willing to contemplate her discharge. We began to understand that she had fled into "health," so to speak—though with plenty of pain and sadness and rage at work well below the surface of her mind. We could only keep our fingers crossed, and hope that somehow, sometime, this bright and energetic young lady would find a way to explore further what had happened to her as a child, that she would not remain at the mercy of all that she feared discovering. When we heard, a year later, that she'd run off—disappeared from the sight of everyone she knew, with no notes left, no phone calls made—we could only shake our heads with that mixture of knowledge and impotence that not rarely characterizes psychiatric work with badly troubled, injured people.

In the midst of my psychoanalytic training, I went into the air force, and was put in charge of a major military neuropsychiatric service—forty-eight beds, a large outpatient unit, and a "liaison" section providing consultation at the request of internists or surgeons concerning patients they regarded as experiencing psychological distress in one way or another, along with their serious medical difficulties. All of us physicians had to put in two years of military service, and I was determined to keep my clinical mind as awake as possible, so I tried to keep a substantial number of patients in treatment instead of getting bogged down in administrative work. Also, as chief of our service, I was the one the base's officers (and their wives) tended to seek out.

One day, a year into my stint, the wife of one of the base's chief officers came to see me. She was worried about her son (aged ten) and her daughter (eight), both having "school problems." I had been trained in child psychiatry, she knew, so would I talk with them and try to figure out what was happening? She went on to describe the boy's shyness, even reclusiveness, his indifference to school, his dislike of teacher after teacher; and the girl's bold and sassy behavior with some teachers, her fearful withdrawal when in the company of others. I met with each of the children four of five times, then with their mother several times. The father made appointments to see me, at my request, but always broke them. I recall even now the trouble I had figuring out what was going on. The boy was taciturn, grumpy, evasive—uninterested, really, in seeing me. His mother had insisted that he come, but his mind was elsewhere, I thought, when we were together: he looked out the window, or kept his head bowed, his eyes scanning the floor of my office. Moreover, he kept requesting that I repeat myself—to the point that I asked him whether he was hard of hearing. As for the girl, she announced outright that she was seeing me to oblige her mother, but would do so only for a brief spell. She was doing quite well, she wanted me to know, and had no idea why she should come to see me at all. Yes, she was a poor student—but so what! I still remember my sense that this girl was fresh, tough, all too self-possessed, and rather unlikable. By our third session she was grim-faced and quite irritated with me: why was I asking her all those questions about her life?

In the end, I concluded that these two had no interest in seeing me, and that I'd best tell their mother so, and perhaps find out what difficulties *she* was having that prompted her to be so worried about her children; they struck me as not all that smart, and hence understandably not greatly interested in the school they attended, a far from superior Mississippi public school of the late 1950s. But the mother was not about to let our discussions center on her. She insisted that there was "something wrong" with her children, and she begged me to see them until I found out what that something was. I recall noting her way of putting the matter—of regarding me as a detective of sorts—and I recall telling her that I could be only as useful or effective as my patients desired me to be, and not useful at all when they were disinclined even to meet with me, let alone explore their troubles. Finally, just when I thought we were ending the last of our meetings, the mother broke down, cried and cried, and said there was "more" to be told, but she didn't know whether she would be able to muster the strength to admit what had to be admitted if the family was to begin getting the help she believed it needed. I told her I'd be glad to help, if she wanted to begin sharing some of what she obviously had in mind, but now she stopped talking and seemed lost in a world of reverie, or maybe (I began to realize) of fear and anxiety. Her hands were working all too hard on the handkerchief she had been using to wipe away her tears, and her head was sunk, almost, in her bosom—a melancholy sight indeed.

After that day, much to my surprise, she didn't come back. I had expected her either to make an appointment for the following week or to sit on her troubles for a while and then return either to discuss them forthrightly or at least to keep open the option of doing so on some future occasion. Instead, the story of her and her children slowly faded from my mind, replaced by the stories of the patients I saw, one after the other, in that modern air force hospital. Only in retrospect, in the light of subsequent encounters with other patients, did I develop a suspicion of what might have been upsetting her.

About six months later, a pediatrician who worked at the hospital, a good friend of mine, called me at home on a Saturday evening. He had just seen a boy, the son of an officer, who had fallen off his bicycle and had multiple bruises. The father, who had brought the boy in, had been affectionate to the child, solicitous of his health, yet the doctor was perplexed, maybe even suspicious: the boy did have a knee injury compatible with a fall from a bicycle, but he also had some notable bruises on his upper back, and some evidence of fading bruises there (a yellowing of old black-and-blue marks), as if this was not the only time he had fallen. In fact, the doctor told me, the location of the various bruises didn't at all fit the story of a bicycle fall. But he had hesitated to make any inquiry. He had attended to the injuries, sewed up the boy's knee wound, sent him and his father home.

Now, on the phone with me, he was going over what he had seen, trying to make sense of it, and—I began to realize—asking for some help in the face of a considerable suspicion that something was awry. Resorting to a phrase many of us drafted doctors used rather often, my friend described the father as a strong, tough, blunt-spoken "military type." I asked him to tell me what he thought had happened, as opposed to what he had been told. "I don't know," he said two or three times—then silence. I pushed. I asked him to guess. Finally, he said he believed the boy had indeed fallen from his bicycle, causing a fairly serious knee injury, hence the visit to the hospital. But my friend also said that he believed the boy did not get his other injuries that way. In fact, he had discovered those injuries by accident: "I asked the boy to turn in a certain direction, and he did, but he was in pain, and I asked him where the pain was located, and he denied any pain. I had seen him in quite a lot of pain, though—so I told him he had to take off his shirt, because I needed to give him a shot and I wanted to examine him more thoroughly, 'all over' I said. The boy was reluctant. He looked at his father. The father asked me why I was being so 'curious.' I didn't know what to make of that! It was then, naturally, that I did become curious! I told the father, 'I'm a doctor, and all I want is to be of help.' If they wanted to go someplace else for their medical care—fine. He stood there, staring at me and then at his son. This guy is a weirdo—I knew it on the spot. I knew there was something wrong—something real bad wrong!"

The father told the doctor to go ahead. The doctor made his discovery, and wondered what in the world to do next. Here were a major and his son in a hospital room in Mississippi in 1960. No wonder the doctor wanted to talk to a psychiatrist, wanted to put on record what he had seen and heard, what he knew—though what to do was another matter entirely. In that regard, I was of no great help. We both wanted to go after that air force officer, even as this clinical problem reminded me of what I had gradually begun to suspect was happening in the family of the woman I had seen months earlier. We went to see a lawyer, a lieutenant in the air force who handled legal matters on the base. We dictated our medical statements, edited them, brought them back to him. The young lawyer was quite discouraging, however. He kept talking of "surmise," of the "guesswork" involved; and he kept warning us of the difficulties we would have in attempting to prove what we suspected, to take legal action, to do so in the air force. Not that we would have fared any better outside the air force: here was a respectable member of the bourgeoisie, a person of authority and education and power and means, a person whose son seemed utterly attached to him, ready to do his bidding, say what he wanted said, act as he wanted him to act; and so far as we knew, the major's wife was similarly inclined. Under such circumstances, we seemed to be skeptical outsiders, with an enormous burden of proof on our shoulders, and we had no encouragement or incentive to persist in a medical or legal initiative.

Nevertheless, we did keep trying to find out more, to engage ourselves with the major and his son, with the boy's mother—only to be rebuffed. We called; we sent letters, ostensibly to follow up the boy's medical progress. But he was never brought back to us, even to have the sutures removed from his knee. We assumed the father had taken his son elsewhere—further reason for us to wonder what was really happening to that boy. In time, my pediatrician friend and I gradually began to forget this particular episode, but we remained aware of the moral dilemma confronting us: what does one do when a child appears to be in jeopardy at the hands of a parent, and all one has to go on is a doctor's observations in an emergency room?

A month before I was to be discharged from the air force—by then, 1961, I had started observing black children initiate school desegregation in nearby New Orleans, against great odds—a woman came to see me, the wife of an officer. Though only in her late thirties, she struck me as grandmotherly in appearance. She had a lot to tell me, she let me know—and then clammed up completely. She sat there, in front of my desk, weeping, wiping her eyes, weeping some more. I wondered what to do. I offered tissues. I suggested a cup of tea. I sat in silence. I asked if she might want to tell me what was making her cry. But all to no avail. She stopped crying, resumed crying, said no to my offer of tea, and told me nothing. By then I was watching the clock. I had my scheduled patients; and anyway, I would soon enough be out, no longer an air force doctor. That was what I found myself actually telling her: I would soon be gone, and there were other doctors she might want to see instead. We struggled through another ten minutes. She cried some more. She tried to tell me why she was there, still without success.

This woman did, finally, convey to me that her husband was an air force officer, that they had four children, two boys and two girls, and that she thought her "whole family" ought be there. As I began to ask why, she suddenly stopped crying, worked at composing herself, and much to my surprise, got up, told me she had to go, and within seconds, was on her way out the door. But she did exclaim this: "The children are being beaten up." I followed her, wondering what to say. I wanted to pull her right back into my office, sit her down, get my tape recorder going, and put a series of questions to her. I was convinced that yet again I was learning something important about the abuse of children—though still with no clear mandate to take action. I wanted to call a lawyer, get him over. But the mother was now walking hurriedly, and within seconds was at the elevator door. When the elevator did not appear at once, she turned toward the stairs, and went down them fast. I followed, telling her that I was concerned—indeed, deeply troubled—about what she had just said, that I appreciated fully how hard it would be for her to talk about "certain matters," but that "we really ought to do so."

She would have none of my solicitations. She raced toward her car, in spite of the hot and humid day and the distance involved. I followed, by that time wishing a policeman were near. But what would I have done then? Ask for the arrest of this reasonably sane, well-to-do suburban housewife who had come to the hospital to talk with a doctor and then had a change of mind? At the car, she fumbled in her pocketbook for her keys, while I made a last-ditch effort to be persuasive, to gain at least a few moments of talk right there. She would have none of my pleas, however. Away she drove, while I stood there, a bit surprised at myself: that I'd followed her so relentlessly, tried so vigorously to gain her ear, her agreement to go back to my office and start over again.

Later, of course, I was on the phone. Later, I was hearing another legal lecture—mainly on the futility of any further action on our part. "Wait her out," the lawyer told me. But what if she never returns? I wondered. "That's her right," I was told. But what of those children? I wondered. "They are *hers*," I was told, with the reminder, emphatically stated: "She is not a criminal! She has the right to be left alone, unless you have some compelling reason to interfere with that right." *Some compelling reason*. I kept remembering that phrase, until a day came when I was no longer an air force doctor.

I left the air force for another life, but my pediatrician colleague had another year to serve. We occasionally met at Tulane School of Medicine conferences. I was living in New Orleans, and taking courses at the New Orleans Psychoanalytic Institute. And I was watching a kind of terrible social violence unfold, the mobs that heckled and threatened four little black six-year-old girls, who had been selected to initiate school desegregation in two elementary schools, both totally boycotted by white parents and their children. I wondered how such street violence would affect those youngsters—and was surprised at how well they did. True, they faced constant danger, but they were doing something very valuable, and they knew it. They were enduring threats and the expressed rage of hundreds of men and women, who every day assembled in front of those schools, but these four children possessed something important indeed—a moral purpose, one which meant a lot to them, to their families, and to many others, the world over.

One day I was scheduled to give a talk to my psychiatric and psychoanalytic colleagues on violence and children, an effort to explain how these vulnerable children, every day faced with a mob's obscene shouts and threats, and every day escorted to school by armed federal marshals, nevertheless managed to survive psychologically rather well. A couple of hours before I was to deliver the lecture, I received a call from my former air force colleague; he was going to attend the lecture, and wanted to meet with me afterward. But he could not wait until then to give me some news: the mother I had seen a month before my discharge had returned to the hospital, to see him. Once again she had sat there crying, but eventually she

23

announced that she had to tell someone what was happening in her home, and she knew that he, a pediatrician was the one with whom she ought discuss the matter. "It's what we both suspected," my friend told me, and briefly, he relayed a grim story of a father's brutish assaults on his children in the name of "discipline," and an equally grim story of his sexual involvement with one of his daughters, by then almost a teen-ager. This latter behavior had just been discovered by the mother: the daughter had told her that the father "petted" her sometimes, on the excuse that he "needed" her; he did this particularly after he had shouted at her for one or another supposed transgression. She and her brothers had their chores to do, and he, a martinet, watched closely as they attempted to accomplish them. In some instances, he hit the boys hard for their "failures"; in other instances, he threatened the girl with "punish-ment," then fondled her "on second thought." She had submitted until a week or so before, when she ran away from home and called her mother from a friend's house; her mother had then gone to see the doctor.

When I talked to my colleagues that evening, I couldn't help contrasting the two kinds of violence—a white mob's toward black children, and a parent's toward his sons and one of his daughters. We all agreed that the former, in all its melancholy daily persistence, was somehow less damaging than the episodic outbreaks of the latter. Nothing in the work I have since done has changed my mind on that score. Those black children experienced plenty of danger and fear, heard many insults and threats, went to school in emptied classrooms—yet survived handily; they became heroes to their own people, and to many others. As for those children whose fate my friend had recently come to know, neither he nor I would ever really be able to understand in full what would happen to them. The mother eventually refused to press charges. My friend had not taped their interview, and in a second visit she retracted most of what she had said: "I have a wild imagination, and it gets the better of me sometimes!" My friend could not believe what he heard, nor could I when he repeated her words to me on the phone. Both of us were ready to go personally to that home, to confront the father, even to make a citizen's arrest of him. *Our* imagination was all worked up, I suppose: our moral imagination was challenged by an absolute medical and psychiatric and legal impasse. A few months later the father was transferred to another base, out west, and we two could only talk about how much we had learned, how frustrated and saddened and worried we had been, how angry we still felt toward the father, but also toward his wife, the mother of those children. Nor did labels such as "sadomasochism" help us all that much as we contemplated the kind of daily hell those children must have experienced, never quite knowing what would set their father off; never quite knowing what they ought do, ought not do, in order to spare themselves his angry brutishness, his seductive brutishness; never quite knowing whether their mother's apparent acquiescence meant that she too was a victim, or that she was a second, all-too-willing judge of them and their overall worth as human beings.

We don't really know how many children are beaten up every year by their parents, or are sexually abused at home. In 1974, almost fifteen years after the experiences just described, certain states began requiring doctors, nurses, social workers, teachers, to report instances of child abuse. As such state-mandated requirements became more and more widespread, there was a marked increase in the reported frequency of occurrence of child abuse in the nation. In 1976 some 6,000 *confirmed* cases of abuse were recorded; between 1976 and 1985 over 113,000 cases were identified. The total number of reported cases is of course somewhat higher; many who work with abused children and their families acknowledge that some accusations (perhaps 10 percent) are false, and that some accusations (perhaps 20 percent) simply go unverified, unsupported by concrete evidence.

As for the so-called "psychodynamics" of child abuse, whether specifically sexual or characterized by assault, I go back in my mind to a comment I heard Anna Freud make in 1977, when I talked with her about which psychological stresses children usually manage to survive, and which stresses they find difficult to endure. She was pointing out that though some of the terrible hardships I had known children to experience—the extreme poverty, say, of Brazil's *favela* children or our own migrant farm children—are by no means conducive to a solid emotional life, they are "as nothing to the overwhelming devastation a child experiences when a parent attacks him or her." Of course, she was not then talking about the ordinary discipline we all want for our children, and they surely need. She had in mind quite something else: "These are children who experience the full brunt of their parents' instinctual life— unmediated by conscience, sometimes, or distorted by virtue of a severely disturbed conscience. These children know severe beatings, often directed at a certain part of the body—a part that means something to the parent, we find out in the few cases we have been able to investigate psychoanalytically. Some parents are directing sexual violence at their children; others are carried by aggressive instincts into a 'tantrum,' and the child becomes the object of such rage. It is the worst thing a child can go through, an assault not only on the flesh but on the entire structure of the mind. A girl told us she felt 'swept away'; and by the time she saw us, she was convinced that she would never again regain the major part of herself lost after such repeated experiences. At our staff meetings [of Anna Freud's children's clinic in Hampstead, England] we all struggle with language—we grope for words to express the horror the child feels, the devastation. One analyst spoke recently of an 'ultimate betrayal'; another spoke of 'psychotic behavior on the part of parents, making for a psychotic process in the child.' But I still think the *children* are best at saying what happens—though many will, naturally, not want to say anything at all for a long time, and that may be the most devastating 'statement' of all, the reduction of the child to a mute, paralyzed silence. One girl told us, 'I don't know how to speak of what happened.' Instead, she drew us a picture of a black sky, and a huge tree that had cracked and fallen on the smallest of animals, which she identified as a squirrel. It was her, we knew right away—a devastating picture: the arbitrary action of nature, of male libido in this case, as it 'befell' a poor, vulnerable child who in her own mind had become a pitiful little animal, who tried to run away and tried to 'squirrel away' what strength and individuality she had in her; who tried to nibble away at life, furtively; but who kept being squashed (killed, I guess we should say) by the enormous trees of a forest that seemed constantly to have it in for her. Terrible! Terrible beyond the word *terrible*, I fear."

Later she would spell out just how "terrible" such an assault on a child can end up being. The terror-struck child won't forget what has happened, has a hard time ever shaking off the extreme violation of his or her humanity. Years later that violence lives all too influentially— repeated on a child of the next generation, or sought out by someone who has known nothing else, it seems, and so is destined to be victimized until the last breath. In this regard, I remember several troubled youths whom I treated years ago, among them an angry young man who at seventeen had begun beating up his girlfriend because he needed to act in such a manner if he was to be sexually "successful." Both the young man and his girlfriend, an eighteen-year-old woman who was all too willing to be insulted, emotionally manipulated, and finally, slapped on the face and even beaten severely, had themselves been beaten regularly as children. "Child abuse" thus turns out to be the transmission of violence across the generations. "Identification with the aggressor," seen in so many who have been abused, means this: a child assaulted by a parent is stripped of self-respect and hope and trust, and with no other choice available resorts to the most primitive and elementary (and humiliating) of strategies—copying what the big monster does, or copying the only situation one has known, the situation in which monsters arbitrarily, callously, rule.

Still, there are victims who somehow escape such a fate, and they certainly ought be mentioned: children who have been treated cruelly, hurtfully, children who have been knocked around, maybe sexually assaulted or frightened into one or another sexually compromising situation, but who nevertheless find their way in later life to friendships and affections that are free of abuse and violence. Some individuals manage such a seeming miracle—manage a hard and demanding psychological growth—through the help of psychologists and psychiatrists and social workers, or through the help of pediatricians or teachers or school counselors, or through the help of the clergy, or, not least, through the help of school friends or relatives of boyfriends or girlfriends.

I recall treating a girl whose boyfriend told her that he was afraid to get close to her because, he said, he feared a "devil" inside himself. He was reluctant to discuss the matter— only wanted to sever outright and abruptly a friendship, a closeness, that had been growing and had seemed headed toward marriage. Needless to say, there was a good deal of hope in the mere fact that the young man could have such a discussion, trying thereby to distance his abusive side from himself (by calling it a "devil" within) and from his girlfriend, whom he obviously wanted to love without feeling himself driven to be punitive and mean-spirited.

My patient was all too naive, for a while, hopeful her affectionate devotion to this young man would of itself prove redemptive. One evening they had what seemed to be a minor squabble. Instead of letting things quiet down, my patient tried to get close to her boyfriend: "I wanted to reassure him—let him know how much I loved him. I tried to hold him. I guess I was holding him too tight. Suddenly he went crazy. He broke away from me. He started shouting and screaming. He punched the wall—again and again. It was awful! He got a bloody fist. Then, just when I thought he was quieting down, just when I thought he'd be allright, he came closer and closer (I thought he wanted to make up!) and he came at me with his right hand. He didn't use his fist, no. [I had asked.] He slapped me, real hard. I couldn't believe it! I thought I was dreaming, having a nightmare. I didn't even cry. I didn't say anything. I just stood there. I was in a daze. My mind was a blank. I can even remember staring at the television. He'd turned off the noise before he slapped me. [I asked her what she thought accounted for that action.] I don't know why, I don't.

"It was awful. After the first slap he became a different person. I'd never met this man before! The look in his eyes—he was wild. I know its corny to say it, I know everyone says it, but there was an animal. I didn't talk. I wasn't even scared then. I don't know what happened to me. He was like an animal, but it's as if I'd become one, too. I wasn't judging him, and I wasn't trying to escape. You know what? It's a hard thing to say, but I felt, like, excited. I could feel my face, it was almost wanting to put on a smile. I think it was how worked up he was— that was it: he was really turned on, excited, and I guess it got infectious. He slapped me, maybe five or six times. I started counting, then I even fogged out that way, too; my brain was dead. Yes, I'll admit—if he'd wanted sex, then, I'd have gone along. For a few seconds I thought he *did*. But all of a sudden he changed, he was back to himself. That's when he moved away from me, and he stared at his hand [the one he'd used to hit her], and then he began crying. He didn't make a sound, no. [I had asked.] It was silent—his eyes filled up, and the tears came out, a lot, and his face, his cheeks, they were all wet. I wanted to go hug him. I felt so sorry for him. It was so strange, because he knew. He told me, 'Don't come near me.' He wasn't shouting. He was being sweet, the way he said it. It was as if he was my friend again, and he wanted to help me, and he knew if I came close—like before—we'd be in the same trouble, so he gave me the advice."

There was much more said, then and in other sessions, but even these remarks by themselves tell so very much, I believe—about the shared nature, so often, of abuse, and about the struggle of someone to free himself of his wild, assaultive craziness, something set in motion by closeness, by what others would regard as the pleasures of intimacy but he felt as an all-too-unnerving reminder of a childhood marred constantly by a particular species of child abuse. Months later, my patient at last began to understand what her boyfriend had experienced as a child: "He'd see his father move toward his mother as if he was being friendly, and then he'd go nuts and beat her. He'd beat the kids, too. They'd never know how to read his face! He'd have this mysterious look on it, and you didn't know if he was feeling good or feeling bad, and if he was going to be friendly, or beat you up! It was as if—as if he wanted to do both at the same time."

Fortunately, this man already had enough control to handle at least somewhat his fits of temper. He slapped rather than punched; at a certain point he withdrew; and he was able to signal his girlfriend so that she would not act in a way that would set him yet again irrationally on the attack. In due course, he responded to her suggestion that he seek out a psychiatrist, not a decision made by many abusive individuals. In the long run these two would separate, but I had the distinct impression that the boyfriend was gradually gaining both self-understanding and self-control. Meanwhile, I was talking with my patient about her own interest in this man, her willingness to put up with his assaults repeatedly. Not the least of her childhood traumas involved an abusive mother. Eventually memories of awful moments in the kitchen came to my patient's mind: "My mother was a nervous woman. She was hard for us to figure out. She'd be happy one minute, and then she'd flip. Sometimes she'd go nuts while she was cooking. Something would burn, and she'd shriek. Something would spill, and she'd lose her temper. When she'd be cutting up the onions, she'd start crying, like everyone does, only she'd not stop, she'd go on and on, and then she'd turn on us. Would she! She'd be crying from the onions—and suddenly she'd start hitting us, for no reason at all. She'd start screaming, too—and you couldn't understand alot of what she was saying. She'd be talking about her own childhood. She'd be mentioning her mother and her father, and then she'd switch and remember something one of us did wrong, months ago. Before she was through, she'd have hit every one of us [there were four children], sometimes bad, real bad, sometimes not so bad.

"We felt sorry for her. I can even remember thinking—I was only a kid of seven or so— that we were helping her out that way, that the least we could do was let her go and do it, and then she'd stop and calm down; and you know, afterwards she'd always be just a little extra-nice to us, and we knew why. She'd make those delicious brownies, or some chocolate-ship cookies, and we'd feast on them, and it was a big relief, and it was as if the tension had been building in her, building and building—all our troubles [the family was very poor, and the father had been injured at work and was unemployed], and now we'd helped her 'let loose.' That's what we used to say; that's how we referred to what happened: mother let loose again! I can even remember being *glad* that she was hitting me! It was strange! It was crazy, I realize that now; but when you're a child you don't think of your life as crazy, do you? It's the only life you've ever known, and you're only a few years into it, and there are these big, big people called parents, and they know everything, and whatever they say or do *must* be right—or so you think for a while, until you get older and go to school and start realizing there are other ways to do things, and other people, other grownups, who are different."

I thought of her, I thought of others like her, as I looked at these men and women and children, these fellow American citizens, these fellow human beings, whom a talented and sensitive and determined and thoughtful photographer, Pamela Fong, has enabled us to meet: people who have gone through their own terrible trials and tribulations; people who have witnessed violence being done to others, who have experienced violence, who remember in some part of their minds what patients keep telling people like me. Again and again I hear those patients recall the sudden turn of things, the sudden disruption of a life, the sudden experience of an assault, the sudden pain, the hurt, and worst of all, that feeling of utter disorder and perplexity and confusion, as if the world itself had ceased having any reliable continuity or meaning, as if the ordinary hope that one day will follow another (for a while at least, for the stretch of a life) had now been taken away, and instead one faced a kind of awful spasm of bluster and turbulence, of convulsion and uproar and frenzy and explosion—the fat in the fire, the devil to pay, an agitator or terrorist wildly on the loose. The result, of course, is more and more human suffering, and not rarely, the possibility that a new recruit to such human degradation will be enlisted. No wonder, then, that patients like the one I have just quoted go through stormy spells while seeing doctors, while putting into words what they long ago experienced, but also become grateful indeed for the life they begin to live thereafter—the spoken words having been an exorcism of sorts, some will remark. One hopes a similar response may have arisen in some of those who appear in these photographs—an important moment of recognition and affirmation that marks a turn in a life, a turn toward self-understanding, and self-acceptance, and soon enough, a kind of peace: days and weeks and months and years unmarked by the assaults once inflicted so randomly, so unjustly.

PHOTOGRAPHS OF THE SURVIVORS AND THEIR FAMILIES

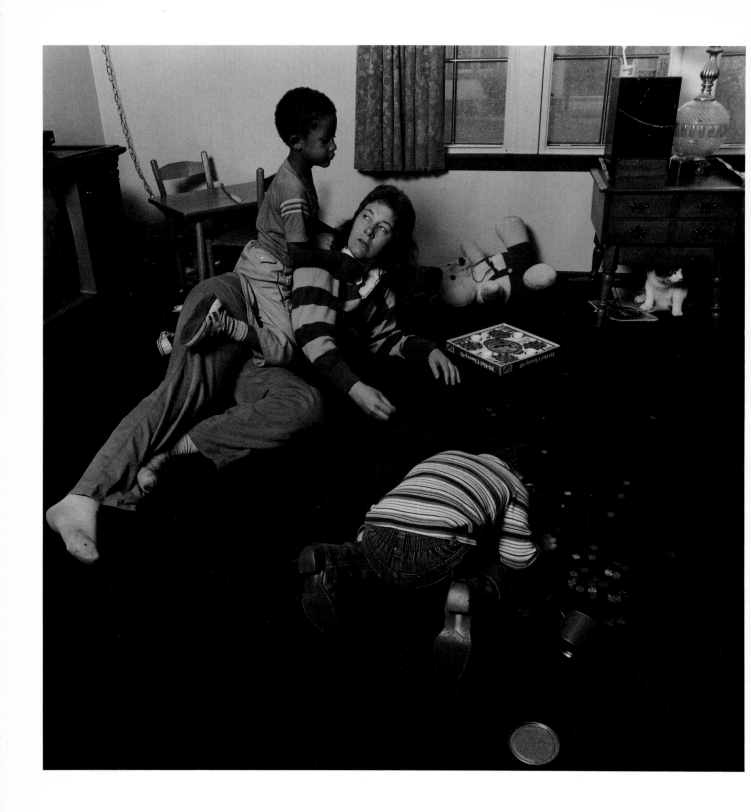

CLINICIANS' TRANSCRIPTS

A twelve-year-old child can, when overpowered, create a fantasy, rationalization, or imaginary world to protect his sanity, by making sense of it. But a baby does not have the rational process which helps cope with trauma or the pain or fear involved.

———————

When you're young, you think that your parents are omniscient. So if you know that and think about children in day-care centers, they're two and three and four years old. It's very easy for these perpetrators to make these children believe that if you go home and you tell mommy and daddy about what we're doing here, I'm going to know it. Like Santa Claus, I'll know everything that you do. I can see you everywhere. And if you tell, I'm going to cut your head off like I did to this bunny rabbit right here in front of you. Or I'll do this to your mommy or daddy. And the kids don't tell. They're terrorized and they think that they'll know if they tell.

———————

They would do a mock operation on the children. And when they wake up, they tell the kids that they put wires inside them and if they tell anybody, their heart was going to explode and it would explode their parents and anybody they loved around them. It was a bomb they put in their heart. And the kids would cry and say they were hurt deep down inside.

———————

And then what's sad is, supposedly when they tell, it's over. But the grief is just beginning because then they have to deal with the split-up family. They have to deal with the guilt. They have to deal with telling fifteen people in having the story told, with having others look at them and whisper and say, Do you know? Then they have to go to the court system. I feel for the kids. It's a nightmare. They will have wished they never told. And that is truly sad. It's a punishment to tell.

———————

They will unconsciously pick out intimate relationships that will duplicate intimate relationships they had with the perpetrator.

It's on an unconscious level that they are seeking the kinds of interactions that are familiar to them, that they were familiar with, that gave them the only kind of love that they got, whatever affection or attention they got through the abusive relationship. That's all they know, so they look for that because that's what's most familiar to them. Even though it may again become an abusive relationship, it's still comfortable in a way. We're all more comfortable with what's familiar than what's not familiar to us.

They don't consciously pick someone who's going to molest their children. It's just that they have the same characteristics and the same type of interactions.

I know that the issue that comes up with the boys individually is that more often, as a result of their abuse, they will turn around and become abusive to younger boys. I just don't see that in as many females. I've seen it a couple of times. I don't know if it's hormones or probably has to do with our culture, in that boys just turn things outward and take their feelings out on other people. They don't get sad, they get mad. They become victimizers to overcome being victims.

Or they victimize themselves. I see a lot of self-mutilation, cutting themselves, burning themselves, suicide attempts, turning to prostitution, drug and alcohol abuse. Most anything to victimize themselves.

They cut themselves . . . they numb themselves. They numb their whole bodies so that they don't feel the cuts. They cut themselves repeatedly. One woman I've known sticks straight pins into herself, and at one point had forty straight pins stuck. It was like a zipper up her arm. Or she would stick one or two pins in so deeply into her upper arm that they were embedded, and we couldn't get them out.

She would numb herself enough so that she couldn't feel forty pins being stuck into her; then she didn't feel any of the emotional pain that she was trying to escape because she can't tolerate the pain, and the pictures constantly coming into her mind. And when she numbs herself and does this, the pictures go away. And that's what she hopes for.

There is a physical and emotional release when they see the blood pouring out of them. They feel better. They feel compelled to cut themselves. And then when they see the blood, they relax and are calmer.

One woman described, as a young child, how both her brothers would molest her every possible way, and both of them ejaculated into her at the same time. She felt like they were putting monsters into her, and even as an adult, she felt like she had monsters inside of her and that cutting herself is one way of letting the monsters out.

———————

He's saying, I'll be good, I like your smile, don't hit me. Literally, he's just saying "Hello." But the message is, I know you're going to hit me. I'll be real good. And here I am. I ran real quick. I didn't go hide. I'll be your friend. Tell me what to do.

———————

The thing these people lose is the ability to trust, to really hold it. They can do the social skills. They can even get into or at least towards intimacy. They can have some sense of loyalty. But they can't trust that someone is going to be there for them, not as well as if their life had been different.

———————

To be able to speak out publicly about what happened to them, they are breaking the ultimate barrier of silence; and by doing that you are letting them know, and yourself know, that you have nothing to be ashamed about. And you are putting the blame where it belongs.

———————

I remember one kid at the centre that they called Monster Hands, horrible name. Beautiful child, but her mother put her hands when she was three in boiling water. So they're just horrible. And she was always getting dressed up because the social worker was going to take her to potentially adoptive families. She'd always try to hide her hands. And you'd see this child all excited, hoping that she looked great in the best, single dress she owned, waiting for the social worker, who was often late, to take her to some place that might like her enough to give her a home. That is grim. And then you see her at night and she's back. And she's devastated. You know, they wanted a younger child or they wanted someone, you know. . . .

———————

When you finally get to the point of some sexual activity occurring between them, it again won't usually be violent. It doesn't have to be forced. And very frequently, her body will respond to the touches. They have orgasms and so she then feels like she must want this to be happening to her. Her body is responding to the touching; and in her later years, it makes her feel very guilty about that, that her body betrayed her. If she really didn't want it to happen then she really wouldn't have responded to the touching. And it takes a lot of time for them to be able to talk about that and a lot of work to undo those feelings. And they feel very humiliated by that, by being betrayed by their own bodies.

And then it's such a vicious cycle. That once they felt pleasurable feelings from the incest, then it's harder, how do you ever say no to the perpetrator because you don't have any right to say no. You responded to them and you must want it.

―――――――

They learn to give their father a blow job to get a new dress or to get something that they wanted. Or to let their father go down on them so they could go to the prom.

―――――――

You can do tissue damage and frighten kids and they can be frightened of being close or touching. There are overlaps, but sexual abuse is poisoning the deepest well there is. It's soul murder. It really is.

―――――――

Physical abuse tends to be more out in the open. There is much more secrecy involved with sexual abuse. And there's more guilt involved.

―――――――

I think society, men, tend to lump all their feelings into rage and anger. Its like tube socks, cheap ones, one size fits all. Men have anger to express everything. If you're frightened as a man, you bluster in your anger and you act anger and you threaten people. Men don't seem to get as much training in expressing the variability and the variety of emotions in the same way that women do.

―――――――

We don't see a lot of upper-middle-class kids because the upper-middle-class kids will go to a private pediatrician. The private pediatrician should report [abuse] but does not have to report.

─────────────

Even though I understood it clinically, it always astounded me that when you release a kid from the nursery to his parents, he runs to the abusing parent; you know, he jumps in his daddy's arms. And his dad is the one that threw him on the wall and broke his shoulder blade.

─────────────

That's the person you please. That's the biggest threat in your environment. That's why some people grow up as abused kids, saying, I'll never do that to my kid. And then they end up doing it.

─────────────

It's called identification with the aggressor. And we soak up those things in our environment which really represent the biggest threat to us, emotionally and physically. And then, that's the thing we take into adulthood. So we tend to act out those things we hated as children. And we catch ourselves saying the same thing we swore we would never say. And that's the part that stays; it's imprinted because it has to do with survival and adapting and so on. If you're going to be part of the pack, or tribe, you'd better act like the strongest, worst person there, because that's how you stay alive.

─────────────

Girls frequently will forgive the molester way before they do the mother that didn't provide the protection, sanctuary, understanding, empathy; couldn't anticipate. Why did she bring that man in? And they'll forgive the man.

─────────────

And if someone says to you, "Mom, the man you sleep with, I mean you touch his body, he's touching your body, the man you're right next to, he put his penis in my mouth," where are you going to file that?

─────────────

Many times they are mothers who were molested themselves; and you'd think that they'd be the very ones that would believe their children. But if they haven't faced that issue themselves, and haven't really accepted it as real for themselves, it would mean they would have to deal with their own guilt and anger and sadness and grief of what happened to them. They may not. If they face that it happened to their children, they have to face that it happened to them; and they, a lot of times, just aren't ready to do that or their self-esteem or self-image is so bad that they can't manage on their own. They can't live or survive without this man in their life. So they have to see it in terms of survival. It's hard to understand when you see them with their children, but they may very honestly believe that the child is lying, that the word of a teen-age girl isn't true.

———————

It seems that even those who don't become perpetrators themselves tell me that they are constantly struggling with impulses to hurt people, and that's a problem. And every time they overcome one of those impulses, they have to grieve over what happened to them, and that's hard for them.

———————

Often they are people that are, in an inner way, insecure and immature about some things and have at least in a few areas grave problems with impulse control, with recognizing that what they do has real effects on other people. Sometimes, in certain areas they lack a lot of empathy and that enables them to continue. Also, sometimes, because they derive some satisfaction at some point during that act of perpetration, whatever it is, hitting or sexually molesting, it's a hard thing for them to beat.

———————

Some people believe there are probably as many males who have been molested as females, and there are so many social taboos on not only are you molested, but it's a homosexual molest. So you have a double, you have two taboos, one right on top of the others. Plus males in our society are supposed to be in charge and macho and fight and so on; so the male is being dominated by another male. So you really have three kinds of societal taboos piled up.

———————

SURVIVORS' TRANSCRIPTS

While taking these photographs, I tape-recorded the stories of many survivors and perpetrators. Some of their words follow. These are not necessarily the words of people whose photographs are here in this book.

This is silly, but I'm thirty years old, sleeping with a teddy-bear pillow. But in the middle of the night when you have a nightmare or flashback, it's just good to have something there that you can hold onto and know that it is not going to hurt you.

————————

I think the hardest thing was to lose a childhood, playing with dolls and tea sets and then going to having sex. And I think that that was one of the hardest things and what's so bad is that I still hate that child.

————————

You act as if you have a choice because it makes life more bearable. We don't really want to have sex with our parents, but we want our parents' love . . . but you'd feel like you had sold your soul. So it's not as if it ever becomes a good thing for a child.

————————

People always say, Why didn't you tell anyone when you were little? But how could I? Why should I think that anyone else is going to be better than my parents?

————————

If you really knew about how I had oral sex and about my best friend who I didn't tell you about and my dad and uncle both sodomized me, so then you wouldn't like me anymore.

————————

I just can't get rid of the anger. I've been trying to deal with a lot of the memories of the abuse by my mother. My hatred for her right now is so intense that I don't even know how I can just sit here and call her mother.

———————

Ellen was like five years old. That's my stepdaughter. I started abusing her. I would have sex with her, fondle her. I'd try to have sexual intercourse with her; but she'd always get, say, No. I was too heavy for her. I weighed too much. And that kept on for about three or four years. And then it went on from sexual abuse to physical abuse and verbal abuse. I turn anger into sexual abuse and abuse her. So it—she got like fifteen or sixteen years old, and it got to where we just got into violence. We'd get into fist fights. There was one time I'd tell her she couldn't do something. She'd make me so angry that I'd hit her. She'd fight back, but she'd still lose.

———————

I had a girlfriend. But we never did anything sexual, besides just kids holding hands. We had a couple of chances to, but I never did follow through on it. I was fifteen, and she was about fourteen. And at the same time, there was this neighborhood girl who was like six or seven. There was a time or two when I would just . . . mess with her . . . fondle her, oral sex.

———————

When I was three, my mom was in the hospital, giving birth to my baby brother; and I had upset my father, who is a rageful alcoholic and hated kids. He had a woman in the apartment; and they'd been drinking. And she got upset when I'd come into the kitchen. Well, she left. He, I think, originally just wanted to get me in bed; but he was jerking me around. He started beating me with the belt; and he totally went nuts. And he wound up trying to kill me. It turned into a sexual thing; and he wasn't able to rape me because he couldn't. He was shaking so bad in my memory that he couldn't, that was too complicated an effort. So he grabbed my head; and he did a very violent, very deep oral . . . rape.

———————

Mom always reminded me of winter sunshine because she'd look like she should be warm but she wasn't.

———————

When he chose someone else, when he chose a child and when he chose our child, then I was no longer a woman. I wasn't adequate with him, and I wasn't adequate with my child.

———————

I was abused by a friend of the family from age five to about nine. I've had a lot of problems from this. I hate him, because he's really messed up all of my life. I married a man just like my father that was dominating and controlling, and watched my daughters run away from home. I've never been really able to stand up for my children, much less myself, because I feel so worthless, so used.

———————

I always had this "black hole." I could remember everything in such vivid detail, then there was this void, this "black hole." Then one day I suddenly got this series of pictures. And it was like slides from a projector flashing on the wall or on a screen. They were images, just little bits and pieces, but they were frightening. And I remembered all the details, I remembered all the feelings and I thought, Oh my god, I've made a connection, I've finally made a connection.

———————

I wish I could have a dad again because I feel bad when everyone asks me, "Where's your dad? What's his name? Do you have a dad?" And I just don't know what to say. I remember once my dad got so mad, he stomped on me . . . I don't tell any of the kids. . . .

———————

My dad was basically absent. He was a self-made workaholic and emotionally was just not there . . . and my brother was caught up into oedipal feelings towards my mother. I think the way he chose to carry them out was sexually with me.

———————

I had always believed that my father was perfect. In fact I pretty much split my parents into good and bad. My mother was bad. My father was perfect. And I was responsible for anything that went wrong.

———————————

I'm pretty sure Dad molested Michael too because I would see him go into his room, and I would be terrified for Michael—terrified about going into the room and seeing what was happening.

———————————

I'm your brother, and Dad is having sex with you . . . and I'm supposed to protect you. But that's my dad, and I'm not supposed to. . . . Damn it, bitch. I mean you always got everything. I'm glad you got hurt.

———————————

She must have noticed Dad being gone a lot. And one time, when I was eleven . . . Dad and I were [laughter] getting into the shower and Mom walks in, okay? And all she did was look at us and say, "Well, . . . put your underwear on before you get in the shower." [More laughter.] I just couldn't believe it. We had already had sex. This was really going to help.

———————————

He spanked with black sticks. He used a black stick that left welts. His father hung himself. And his father was beaten in a woodshed until he stuttered. So as you see, it was passed on from generation to generation to generation.

———————————

I'm pretty sure my father was abused too. My uncle told me that my grandmother used to lock him and his twin outside in the snow or in the closet, and afterward, she would take them out and be "hyperaffectionate" with them.

———————————

The biggest investment is that I have three grandchildren that have never been victimized and will probably never be victimized. And that to me makes everything, all the pain, all the things you have to go through to be a survivor, worth all of it. I'd go through it ten more times to make sure that generation is safe.

I remember being upstairs, in bed, listening to the radio. And someone was describing a child abuser and it was in some rather drastic terms. And as I was listening, tears welled up in my eyes because I realized they were describing me. . . . I started thinking to myself, "They would be better off without me."

I know when he asked me not to hit him anymore when he was a little boy. He said, "Mommy, why are you doing this? Please stop." I couldn't stop. I just kept doing it.

When we discovered that my cousin had been molested, my mother said, "Your father would never touch you." And that was the opportunity for me to finally say, "Where were you? . . . where were you when he used to knock the hell out of me, and knock me off the chair at the dinner table?"

BREAKING THE CYCLE

I had a real conviction that the world was quite broken and it was very possible to never really heal. But what kept me going was the fact that it was my duty as a human being to search, to pursue life and healing, and I would just do it. Having gone through it I can now say that there is hope. And healing is possible, and having a regular life with good relationships and a world that makes sense and isn't topsy-turvy is possible, and it comes about by taking small tiny steps whenever and wherever you can and resting a lot.

A large part of healing is learning to be a good parent and knowing when to push your child a little farther and when to tell your child to rest and you're going to take care of him.

It's good to have a model of what it is a good parent does, how they act toward their child, how they try to set up their child for success instead of failure, what understanding means. All that stuff, I had to learn because if you just talk about the ego and the superego, my superego was completely destructive. I needed a new image. I would actually practice being an adult and I would practice being a child and being loved.

———

Confronting my uncle and my husband was probably a lot easier than confronting myself, that many, many times, my own weakness had played into the hands of my uncle and my husband. I had to stop my own vicious cycle of abusing myself and letting people I love be abused. I was forced to learn to take care of my children.

———

I don't think it ever goes away. I don't think it ever leaves you. But I think you could get enough strength to put it into perspective, to a place where it belongs and do normal things and have a normal life, a normal sexual life, a normal emotional life, a normal family life.

———

Given that it was something that went on over a period of time with a close perpetrator, it's probably not anything they'll ever forget. It has altered their lives permanently. Now if they heal, if enough healing occurs, then the alteration may be in a positive way. But they will have to work very hard to get to that point. And there will probably always be little things that can trigger eruptions now and then.

But if they gain enough insight and awareness into themselves, they'll know what's going on. They'll know that seeing a certain movie or smelling a certain smell or something that might go on may trigger a memory that they haven't quite worked through yet or they don't know. Maybe they'll need to go back to see a therapist a couple of times and work through it. Or maybe it's just a matter of doing some reading and writing and working on their own. That can happen periodically throughout their lives. But it will be a shift to where the abuse is no longer in control of them and their lives. They'll be in control. It's just that, now and then, things may pop up that they'll have to deal with. But they're still in control overall.

—————————

The most important type of therapy is group therapy. It is very effective and gives the survivor support. It may jolt you, or you might hear something that resonates within you, which will make you respond. In a group, you can feel safe remembering. And then dealing with it on a private basis would be good. But the support of a group is best.

—————————

You live in silence so long and most of the time you think you are just on your own, but coming into the group, the union and comfort that you feel, the love and compassion that everyone has for you the minute you walk through the door, is something that you're afraid to feel on the street. It is invaluable. You don't have to feel ashamed and humiliated about who you are, and noboby's going to judge you in here.

—————————

Psychotherapy is fine. It's good to understand, but if you've lived a life of deprivation and terror, you don't need to understand as much as you just need to be healed by having someone love you and by learning that the world is not a terrible place, that people are not crazy, that black isn't white and white isn't black. And that most people are fairly consistent and that there are good people in the world.

———————

I wanted the group to be their group, and totally under their control. I'm there to facilitate it and to keep things going but as far as what one person puts into the group or gets out of it, it's under their control. They don't make a commitment to meet, or to facilitate or to be there a certain number of times, so they don't have to feel guilty because getting that control is one of the big issues for adult survivors as is learning how to know what their own needs are and to take care of those needs instead of taking care of somebody else's needs.

———————

A special kind of expertise is necessary to communicate with the inner child, to know how to talk to them and know how to know what they're telling you. And if you don't develop a relationship with that child, you're not going to get anywhere in therapy because that child has to learn to trust you as a therapist, and learn to trust that grown up person that they're living inside of. And they gradually catch up and go through those phases that they didn't get to go through. They work on learning to help that child develop a better image of themselves as a child. They learn how to be a child and how to keep the fun part of the child so they could play and not see themselves as garbage, or just totally worthless, and continue to think that they caused all the abuse. So they develop a healthier view of themselves, so they can maintain the happy playful part of the child. But they must learn to be more aware of it so that when they're in a stressful situation, the child part of them doesn't get triggered and take control and ruin things for them, like the child has been doing for many years. The child takes control of situations where the adult really needs to be in charge.

———————

I think most of the people who have done work with perpetrators don't think that they can really be cured per se, much like alcoholism cannot be cured. But they can learn to keep their behavior under control. They require and have to make a commitment to life-long support groups, much like AA, to keep it under control. They have to work at it constantly. If they are willing to work hard enough to control it and to accept full responsibility for what they did, they could deserve to be reunited with their children. It would have to be a very slow process.

———————

It's necessary to evaluate the state of the child and to make sure the parent knows how to make the child feel safe and that the surroundings of the child remain the same. It's important that the parent maintain a familiarity of things around the child. Don't make drastic changes. Certain things can help the child express himself: sand play, drawings to say how they feel, not necessarily in a verbal way. They have to feel totally accepted. There might be mood fluctuations. They may be difficult, oppositional, saying no to everything. Parents need to know how to cope with them. And a therapist can help both the child and the parent.

———————

Parents feel guilty or to blame for the incident. So when the child acts in an oppositional way or moody or angry, parents have difficulty dealing with it. It's important for parents to have therapy during this time, so they don't react to the child in a way that is not beneficial for the child. Also, it is important that the significant or non-perpetrating parent spend more time with the child during this time, to be more physically present with the child until the child feels confident again.

———————

The most important message to put across to survivors is they were not at fault. The child is not to blame himself or herself. There is no way you could have caused it. Everything that you feel is important.

———————

You need to see that you could change your life, that you don't have to be living the way you've been living, with self-hatred and in a world by yourself. And no matter how old you are, or how young you are, if your life is miserable, you have the power to change it. And it is a struggle. It is hard. There's no minimizing how hard it is. But the glory of what you get when you finish with it, the peace that you have within yourself, the love you have for yourself once the shame and guilt is gone and you're given back what you deserve, is worth all the struggle. And that's what I hope they see.

———————

You can't change what happened to us but hopefully it will keep it from happening to any other kids.

TECHNICAL DATA

Nearly all of the photographs were taken with a Hasselblad camera with Kodak Tri-X 120 film and printed on selenium toned Agfa-Gavaert Insignia or Portriga-Rapid fibre-base paper.